WORLD RELIGIONS
BUDDHISM

BY DON NARDO

Content Adviser:

Roger R. Jackson, Ph.D., Professor and Chair,
Religion Department, Carleton College

Reading Adviser:

Alexa L. Sandmann, Ed.D., Professor of Literacy,
College and Graduate School of Education,
Health, and Human Services, Kent State University

Compass Point Books
151 Good Counsel Drive
P.O. Box 669
Mankato, MN 56002-0669

 This book was manufactured with paper containing
at least 10 percent post-consumer waste.

Photographs ©: Alamy: Kevin Lang 26, travelib china 24; The Bridgeman Art
Library: Bildarchiv Steffens/Rudolf Bauer 22, British Library, London, UK/
British Library Board, All Rights Reserved 15, 21, Dinodia/Private Collection 33,
World Religions Photo Library 13; Getty Images: AFP 4–5, 6, 7, Lonely Planet
Images/John Banagan cover; iStockphoto: Bartosz Hadyniak 29, enviromantic
(pattern design element) cover (middle & bottom), back cover (left) & throughout;
Mary Evans Picture Library 17; Shutterstock: Elena Yakusheva 10, Gina Smith
41, Harald Høiland Tjøstheim 36, Irina Efremova 38, Kaetana 35, Kheng Guan
Toh 8, Luciano Mortula 31, maga (background texture) 4, 13, 21, 31, 37, 46, 47,
Naomi Hasegawa (pattern design element) cover (top & bottom), back cover (top),
1, 45, sidebars throughout, Philip Date 30, Vladimir Wrangel 42, Yanfei Sun 37.

Editor: Brenda Haugen
Designers: Ashlee Suker and Bobbie Nuytten
Media Researcher: Svetlana Zhurkin
Library Consultant: Kathleen Baxter
Art Director: LuAnn Ascheman-Adams
Creative Director: Joe Ewest
Editorial Director: Nick Healy
Managing Editor: Catherine Neitge
Cartographer: XNR Productions, Inc.

Library of Congress Cataloging-in-Publication Data
Nardo, Don, 1947–
 Buddhism / by Don Nardo.
  p. cm.—(World religions)
 Includes index.
 ISBN 978-0-7565-4236-8 (library binding)
 1. Buddhism—Juvenile literature. I. Title. II. Series.
 BQ4032.N37 2009
 294.3—dc22   2009011453

Visit Compass Point Books on the Internet at *www.compasspointbooks.com*
or e-mail your request to *custserv@compasspointbooks.com*

Table of Contents

Chapter One

A TEST OF FAITH

September and October 2007 turned out to be dark and dismal months for Buddhists in Burma, the Southeast Asian nation that lies east of India. Most Burmese devoutly follow Buddhism, one of the world's oldest major religions.

They were deeply disturbed by what appeared to be a government assault on their religion.

The trouble began in August. The generals who run the country's government more than doubled the price of fuel, greatly troubling the people. They were not used to being treated this way. For a long time, Burma had been a democracy. But in 1962 the army overthrew the government and later changed the name of the country to Myanmar. (The new name is not recognized by the United States and many other countries.) Since the overthrow, the dictators have ruled with iron fists. The fuel price increase was only the latest of many harsh policies the generals have forced on the people.

A large number of Buddhist monks decided to protest the increase. These religious leaders live in monasteries. In small, secluded communities, they meditate, pray, and take part in various rituals. But on occasion they make their voices heard in public.

This was one of those occasions. Millions of Burmese had been poor before the price of fuel went up. Now they were rapidly sinking further into poverty and despair. The monks felt they couldn't remain silent about this blow to the people. In

Demonstrators displayed a banner as they marched with Buddhist monks in Rangoon on September 24, 2007. The protest was the strongest show of dissent against the ruling generals in nearly two decades.

September 2007, monks marched through the streets.
They hoped their demonstrations would bring about
a repeal of the price increase and move the country
toward democracy.

*In red robes and with their heads shaved, Buddhist monks marched to
protest the increase in gas prices.*

The monks' well-meaning strategy failed. The dictators responded by ordering a crackdown on the robed protesters. Soldiers attacked and arrested thousands of the monks. At least 20 of the demonstrators were killed and more than 100 were still missing long afterward. The government closed most of the country's monasteries. It also seized large pieces of property owned by Buddhists. The government's actions

Armed police blocked a street in downtown Rangoon as the government tried to crush protests in the city.

 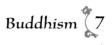

The Shwedagon Temple

The Shwedagon Temple is Burma's oldest Buddhist shrine. According to Buddhist tradition, the original structure was built about 2,500 years ago, but it has been rebuilt several times. The current structure dates to 1769. The temple is topped by an enormous dome and spire. The dome is covered with many sheets of pure gold and decorated with thousands of diamonds and rubies. Monks hold ceremonies inside. Ordinary Buddhists visit the temple to pray and meditate. They also come to see religious relics, including eight hairs said to have belonged to the Buddha himself.

provoked widespread outrage.

Many Burmese were also upset by what happened to the beautiful Shwedagon Temple. Located in Rangoon, Burma's largest city, the temple is the holiest Buddhist site in the country. Soldiers chased away most of the temple's monks. The government installed razor-wire fences around the temple and guarded it with armored vehicles.

News of these events swiftly traveled around the world. Many people in the United States and other Western countries were perplexed. Most residents of Western countries know little about societies and traditions in this part of the world. They wondered why the dictators would attack and jail unarmed, peaceful monks.

In the days and weeks that followed, the world press provided the explanation. The dictators who run Burma have long viewed Buddhist monks as a threat to their authority. The monks have no guns or other standard weapons. Their power is simply their moral influence. But that is too threatening for the generals to tolerate.

The vast majority of Burmese look up to the monks. These holy men steadfastly hold true to Buddhism's beliefs, which were established 2,500 years ago. The faithful believe that at that time the Buddha had discovered life's basic truths. To do this, he had to make many

Buddhist Branches

There are three main branches of modern Buddhism. The largest is Mahayana Buddhism. It has about 240 million followers. Most live in China, Vietnam, Korea, or Japan. Theravada Buddhism has about 100 million worshippers. Most Theravadans live in Sri Lanka, Burma, Laos, Thailand, or Cambodia. Vajrayana, or Tibetan, Buddhism has about 10 million followers. They live mainly in Tibet, Nepal, Bhutan, and Mongolia.

Boys as young as 7 can study to become monks.

personal sacrifices. Later Buddhist monks, including those in modern Burma, have made similar sacrifices daily. In this way they have become respected role models and moral leaders for other Buddhists. Their leadership is what the dictators fear. They want all authority in the nation—legal, moral, and otherwise—to be in their own hands.

This was not the first time Buddhist monks had been

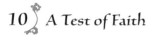

persecuted in Burma. The generals had launched four other crackdowns since 1965. In each case, they arrested many monks and temporarily closed many monasteries.

As in other attacks on Buddhist monks over the centuries, the victims of the 2007 attacks offered no physical resistance. This is because the monks preach and live by the Buddha's teachings and ethical rules. Among these is never to harm a living thing. Buddhists also hold dear a concept called Perfect Action, which urges peaceful conduct at all times. Thus the monks who were beaten and arrested in Rangoon were not acting violently.

These champions of the Buddhist tradition were forced to endure a great deal of rough treatment. Most of those arrested were forced into detention centers. Often so many were packed into a single room that no one could lie down. There were no toilets, and the only food was a little cooked rice. The prisoners were beaten repeatedly. When one of them identified himself as a monk, a guard slapped him and yelled, "You are no longer a monk! You are just an ordinary man with a shaven head!"

Buddhists around the world spoke out against the mistreatment. The crackdown continued. Many people, both inside and outside Burma, said this was a true test of faith. In the face of violence and cruelty, would Buddhists

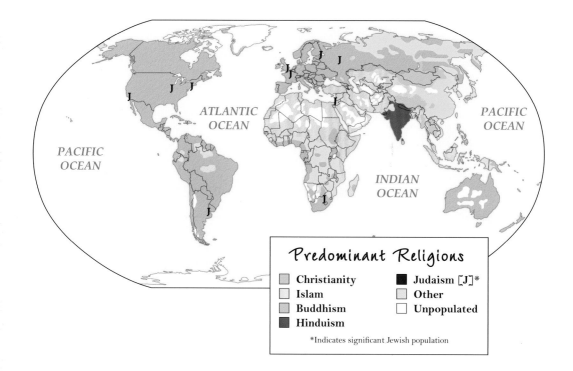

Predominant Religions

- Christianity
- Islam
- Buddhism
- Hinduism
- Judaism [J]*
- Other
- Unpopulated

*Indicates significant Jewish population

remain true to their belief in avoiding violence? It may
be too soon to tell, but for centuries they have never
abandoned their beliefs, so it's unlikely they will change.

Chapter Two

BUDDHISM'S FAMOUS FOUNDER

Many people who know little about Buddhism assume the Buddha is the god worshipped by members of that faith. The truth is that Buddhists do not recognize an all-powerful god. The Buddha was a flesh-and-blood person. He was a teacher and deep thinker.

A painting on the wall of a Korean temple depicts the Buddha seated under a tree in front of his disciples.

13

Dissatisfied with conflict, hunger, and other ills plaguing humanity, he found a way to rise above them. In this way, he found peace and contentment. He taught others to do the same. The Buddha's teachings became a powerful spiritual legacy that has been embraced by hundreds of millions of people over the centuries.

The man who would later be called the Buddha was born Siddhartha Gautama in northern India, in what is now Nepal. Tradition dates the event to 563 B.C.E., but many historians believe he was born a century later.

Siddhartha was a prince, the son of a local Indian king. His father, Suddhodana, wanted the boy to grow up to be a warrior, not a holy man as had been predicted. Hoping to shelter him from exposure to poverty and other human ills, the king confined Siddhartha to the palace grounds. Buddhists believe that as the young

To acknowledge all world religions, Compass Point Books uses new abbreviations to distinguish time periods. For ancient times, instead of B.C., we use B.C.E., which means before the common era. B.C. means before Christ. Similarly, we use C.E., which means in the common era, instead of A.D. The abbreviation A.D. stands for the Latin phrase anno Domini, which means in the year of our Lord, referring to Jesus Christ. Of course not all peoples worship Jesus.

man grew up, he knew nothing about disease, suffering, and death. He got married, became a father, and enjoyed a happy life, just as his father had intended.

At the age of 29, Siddhartha decided he wanted to see what lay beyond the palace walls. Sneaking away, he went into the countryside. There he encountered something he had never seen—a very old man. With a touch of sadness, the prince suddenly realized that all people, including him, must someday grow old. Not

A 19th century Burmese painting depicts scenes from Prince Siddhartha Gautama's early life.

long afterward, he saw two other unfamiliar things. One was a sick person. The other was a dead man. By asking questions, Siddhartha learned that illness was common and that all people eventually die.

Siddhartha was shocked to learn of the existence of human suffering. He now wondered whether life was even worth living. Then he saw a holy man walk by. The monk seemed quite calm and content. The prince learned that monks spend much time alone, in meditation.

Hoping to find the source of contentment, Siddhartha decided to follow the monk's example. He left the palace and his family and adopted a life of extreme self-discipline. He nearly starved himself. After a while, he learned to live on only a few grains of rice each day. This self-denial was meant to help his mind focus on attaining wisdom to become enlightened.

None of these activities worked. Siddhartha learned that abusing himself dulled, rather than sharpened, his mind. So he started eating again. Still eager to learn about the sources of suffering and happiness, he went for a long walk. After a while, he saw a large tree and sat beneath it to shade himself from the sun. He sat cross-legged and put his hands together in his lap. Then he began meditating.

Siddhartha decided to remain under the tree until he reached enlightenment. Through the night, he thought about countless generations of humans suffering. With all the energy he could muster, he searched for a way to overcome this cruel cycle. In the morning, the young

Siddhartha meditated alone to gain enlightenment.

 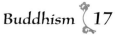

man opened his eyes. On his face was a look of calmness and confidence. He was sure he had achieved his goal of understanding human suffering. Buddhists believe this was the moment he became the Buddha, which means the Enlightened One.

After his enlightenment, the Buddha stayed under the tree for several weeks. His heart was full of peace and joy.

Much of the wisdom the Buddha had gained consisted of basic truths about life. One was that human suffering results from personal greed and self-indulgence. That is, most people think too much about their possessions and too little about justice and happiness for everyone. Fortunately, the Buddha said, these ills can be overcome. So he provided a way of doing so. He created a code of conduct known as the Eightfold Path. It is a series of positive choices people can make to improve both their own lives as well as society.

The Buddha began sharing this newfound wisdom with others. His sharing gained him many followers in northern India. One was a grieving mother named Kisagotami whose baby had died unexpectedly. Kisagotami came to the Buddha and asked him for medicine that would bring her son back to life. The Buddha told her to bring him a handful of mustard seed, but that it must

The Eightfold Path

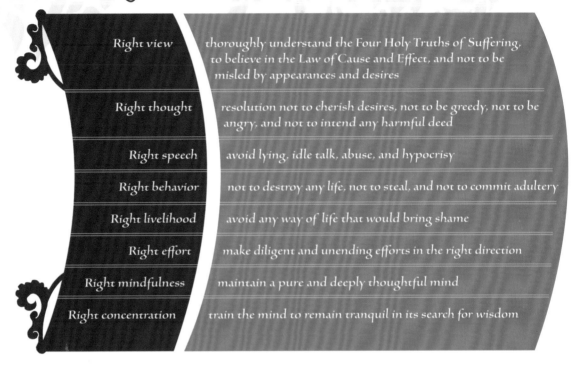

Right view	thoroughly understand the Four Holy Truths of Suffering, to believe in the Law of Cause and Effect, and not to be misled by appearances and desires
Right thought	resolution not to cherish desires, not to be greedy, not to be angry, and not to intend any harmful deed
Right speech	avoid lying, idle talk, abuse, and hypocrisy
Right behavior	not to destroy any life, not to steal, and not to commit adultery
Right livelihood	avoid any way of life that would bring shame
Right effort	make diligent and unending efforts in the right direction
Right mindfulness	maintain a pure and deeply thoughtful mind
Right concentration	train the mind to remain tranquil in its search for wisdom

come from a house never touched by death. Full of hope, the woman went out to search for the mustard seed. Kisagotami went to one house after another. At each home, the people were willing to give her some mustard seed, but she couldn't accept it because each family she visited had at some time experienced the death of a loved one. Kisagotami went back to the Buddha and told him what she had learned. All families experience the sorrow of death. She realized her suffering was shared by everyone.

Another of the Buddha's followers was his son. The boy had heard about his father's feats and proudly adopted the new philosophy.

Many years passed. The Buddha sensed that his death was near. He asked his followers to continue teaching people how to overcome suffering. He also reminded them that each person can help make the world better. The key, he said, is kind, generous thoughts and actions. He believed such behavior would enhance both one's own life and the lives of others.

The Buddha's followers took his lessons to heart. After his death, they began spreading them beyond India's borders. In this way, a major new faith, one based on compassion and hope, took root in human society.

Chapter Three

SACRED TEXTS AND BELIEFS

Like other major religions, Buddhism has holy writings that contain the faith's basic beliefs. But Buddhism has no central sacred text. There are many Buddhist sacred writings. They were originally written in several languages,

A page from a sutra, one of the sacred texts of Buddhism, translated into Chinese

including Sanskrit, Chinese, Tibetan, and Mongolian. The first, containing writings called *sutras* (or *suttas*), are thought to be the actual words of the Buddha. The writings in the second group are histories, commentaries, and quotations by later important Buddhist teachers.

One way that Buddhist texts differ is in how they are viewed by various groups within the faith. For example, Theravada Buddhists accept a restricted, early collection of holy texts as its *Tipitaka* (or *Tripitaka*). The word *Tipitaka* means "three baskets." This reflects the fact that the texts have three main sections. The first, called the *Vinaya Pitaka*, consists of rules for Buddhist monks. It also contains complex explanations of why these rules were made. The second section is the *Sutta Pitaka*. It consists of more than 10,000 suttas (teachings) by the Buddha and his closest followers. The *Tipitaka's* third part is the *Abhidhamma Pitika*, which summarizes the Buddha's teachings.

A tablet with part of the Tipitaka *is kept in a temple in Mandalay, Burma.*

Mahayana Buddhists also view the *Tipitaka* as an important holy writing. Yet unlike the Theravadans, they give another sacred collection equal status. This collection is most often referred to as the *Mahayana Sutras*. It was written between 200 B.C.E. and 200 C.E., long after the Buddha's death. The *Mahayana Sutras* contains more than 2,000 of the Buddha's teachings.

These and other Buddhist sacred texts have survived because of the devotion of generations of monks. For centuries they painstakingly copied and recopied them by hand. Often they received special rewards or blessings for this work.

The Bodhisattvas

One of the most important sections of the *Mahayana Sutras* is the *Lotus Sutra*. It's a long sermon the Buddha is said to have delivered to followers who were in search of enlightenment. In the speech, he emphasizes the beneficial traits of the bodhisattvas— enlightened people who temporarily stop short of attaining the ultimate liberation of nirvana. They choose instead to stay on Earth and help people who are still suffering.

No matter which sacred texts they hold most dear, all Buddhists accept certain basic principles. First, and perhaps most important, is that the purpose of life is to become free from suffering by attaining enlightenment. Also, nothing is permanent. So life always leads to death. Further, all empires and nations, no matter how mighty, are destined to fall.

Another basic belief of Buddhism concerns the existence of God. Buddhists believe that the universe was not

A monk in a Chinese monastery copies Burmese Buddhist text.

created by an all-powerful supernatural being. There is no supreme deity to provide humans with a path to salvation—eternal life after death.

The Buddha taught that each person can find his or her own path to salvation. The key, he said, is to seek wisdom and enlightenment. One can then escape the earthly cycle of life and death. In this cycle, Buddhists believe, when a person who is not enlightened dies, he or she is reborn in another body. The person then endures a lifetime of suffering once again. In contrast, a person who becomes enlightened is freed from this endless, negative cycle. Such liberation is called nirvana. A Buddha is a

Accept Nothing on Faith

One of the Buddha's most profound teachings was that people shouldn't accept ideas only on faith. Instead they should test ideas and see for themselves whether they are constructive. The Buddha said: "Believe nothing, O monks, merely because you have been told it ... or because it is traditional, or because you yourself have imagined it. ... But whatsoever, after due examination and analysis, you find to be conducive to the good, the benefit, the welfare of all beings—that doctrine believe and cling to, and take it as your guide."

 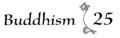

person who has achieved nirvana and fulfills a great historical mission.

In addition, all Buddhists accept and revere the Eightfold Path introduced long ago by the Buddha. The path's right actions, including right thinking and right speech, are examples of how people should behave. The Buddha also listed the major ways that people should *not* behave. They became known as the Five Moral Rules.

According to Buddhist teachings, a person who strictly follows the Eightfold Path and Five Moral Rules is well on the way to achieving nirvana.

One way that Buddhists express their beliefs is through celebrating holidays. Some Buddhist holidays vary from sect to sect and from country to country. The Buddhist New Year is an example. Theravada Buddhists

THE WAY TO NIBBĀNA
NAMO TASSA BHAGAVATO ARAHATO SAMMASAM BUDDHASSA

ALL BEINGS ARE SUBJECT TO SUFFERING. TO MAKE THE SUFFERING END, VIPASSANĀ (INSIGHT MEDITATION CONTEMPLATION) MUST BE PRACTISED. WHEN THE BUDDHA APPEARS IT IS POSSIBLE TO PRACTISE VIPASSANĀ. WHOEVER WISHES TO FOLLOW THE VIPASSANĀ PRACTICE, HE AT FIRST MUST PURIFY HIS SĪLA (MORALITY). DEPENDING ON THE PURIFICATION OF SĪLA, IT IS POSSIBLE TO CULTIVATE SAMADHI. THROUGH THE POWER OF SAMADHI ONE IS ABLE TO CONTEMPLATE THE OBJECT THAT MANIFESTS IN HIS OWN SENSE. WHATEVER MENTAL ACTIONS APPEAR ONE MUST CONTEMPLATE THEM. WHATEVER PHYSICAL ACTIONS APPEAR ONE MUST CONTEMPLATE THEM. WHEN HE CONTEMPLATES MIND AND MATTER, HE SEES THE INDIVIDUAL CHARACTERISTIC. WHEN HE SEES THE INDIVIDUAL CHARACTERISTIC, THE UNIVERSAL CHARACTERISTIC, ANICCA (IMPERMANENT), DHUKKHA (SUFFERING), AND ANATTA (SOULLESSNESS), WILL COME INTO MANIFESTATION. HE SEES MIND AND MATTER AS IMPERMANENT. WHAT IS IMPERMANENT IS SUFFERING, WHAT IS SUFFERING IS SOULLESS. IF HE SEES IMPERMANENCE, HE SEES SUFFERING; IS HE SEES SUFFERING, HE SEES SOULLESSNESS; IF ONE SEES SOULLESSNESS, HE SEES NIBBĀNA. ON SEEING NIBBĀNA ALL KILASAS ARE ERADICATED. BY ERADICATING KILASAS, KAMMA BECOMES CEASED. ON THE CESSATION OF KAMMA THE RESULTS OF KAMMA WILL BE NO MORE. THEN ALL SUFFERINGS ARE IN END. THIS IS THE STATE OF NIBBĀNA A PEACEFUL BLISS.

HOW TO PRACTISE MEDITATION CONTEMPLATION

BE SEATED CROSSED LEG OR ON THE FOLDED KNEES SO THAT TO SIT LONG-LASTING. CLOSE THE EYES AND MIND WHAT YOU FEEL AS MUCH AS YOU CAN. BE MINDFUL THE INHALE AND OUT HALE OR RISING AND FALLING OF THE ABDOMEN. KEEP WATCH AS IT IS THUS; COLD, HOT, PAINFUL, ACHING, ITCHING, WAVERING AND SO ON EVERY ACTION OR MOVEMENT MUST BE MINDFUL EVEN AT THE MOMENT OF EXCRETING AND URINING. WALKING, SITTING, STANDING, LYING, TAKING SOMETHING ETC. ESPECIALLY IN WALKING, IF YOU ARE WELL CONCENTRATED IN STEPPING, CARRY-ON LEAPING AND STEPPING DOWN AND THE LIFTING, LEAPING AND STEPPING DOWN SHOULD BE PRACTISED ALL PERCEPTIONS SUCH AS SEEING, HEARING, SMELLING, EATING, FEELING TANGIBLE THINGS AND THINKING SHOULD BE MINDFUL AT THAT VERY MOMENT. IT IS WHOLE SOME IDEED IF YOU PRACTISE CONTEMPLATION AND IT IS KILESA (DEFILEMENT) IF YOU DON'T. THE MORE THOROUGH YOU PRACTISE, THE MORE CONCENTRATION YOU GAIN. YOU ARE ASSURED TO GAIN THE WISDOM OF RISING UP AND PASSING AWAY OF THE NĀ MA RUPA DHAMMA IN ACCORDANCE WITH THE LAW OF NATURE.

DHAMMA DANA
U THAN HTAIK - DAW AYE MYINT
SAN PYA FAMILY
28TH, BETWEEN 84TH AND 85TH STREET
MANDALAY

- U VATHETHA
(THI-TA-LONE SAYADAW)

An inscription describes how to achieve nirvana.

The Five Moral Rules or Precepts

1. I shall not harm any living thing.

2. I shall not take what does not belong to me.

3. I shall refrain from sexual misconduct.

4. I shall not tell falsehoods.

5. I shall avoid intoxicants.

celebrate it for three days, starting at the first full moon in April. Mahayana Buddhists observe the New Year in January or February. And Tibetan Buddhists celebrate it in February or March.

Whatever the date, worshippers from all of these sects visit their Buddhist temple. There they give food to the monks and the poor. Ceremonies include walking around the temple three times, chanting, and meditating. Meditating is said to let the worshipper achieve a state of calmness and contentment. It also allows the person to think about and better understand the truths of life, including the nature of suffering.

The most important Buddhist holiday is Vesak,

Buddhist Symbols

Buddhists recognize many symbols of their faith. Especially important in Tibetan Buddhism are the Eight Auspicious Symbols:

Parasol (umbrella)	stands for royalty and spiritual power
Golden fishes	stand for good fortune
Treasure vase	stands for spiritual and material abundance
Lotus flower	stands for mental and spiritual purity
Conch shell	stands for the fame of the Buddha's teachings
Endless knot	stands for the Buddha's great wisdom
Victory banner	stands for the triumph of knowledge over ignorance
Wheel	stands for the Buddha's teachings

which honors the Buddha's birthday, his enlightenment, and his death. Theravadans celebrate Vesak during the first full moon in May, but Tibetans usually observe it in June. Japanese Buddhists celebrate the Buddha's birth April 8 and his enlightenment December 8.

Another important celebration, Sangha Day, takes place during the first full moon of the third lunar month, which is usually at the end of February or beginning of March. It honors the memory of the Buddha's visit to an important monastery in Rajagaha, India.

On Vesak, Sangha Day, and other Buddhist holidays, worshippers visit their temples, make food offerings, and meditate, as they do during the New Year's festival. During Vesak some Buddhists also release small animals or caged birds as an act of generosity and to symbolize the Buddha's compassion for all things. Some bathe small Buddha idols in remembrance of the Buddha's birth.

A monk prays inside a temple.

Buddhists also practice other rituals during holidays and in ordinary worship. For example, sacred sounds called mantras are important to many Buddhists. They are especially important to Tibetan Buddhists. The most common mantra is a chant. The worshipper repeats the phrase "Om mani padme hum," meaning "Praise to the jeweled lotus," over and over, often while meditating. Tradition holds that repeating this and other mantras protects the worshipper from evil, illness, and misfortune.

Many Buddhists use hand gestures called *mudras*

A Tibetan man with his prayer wheel and beads

during worship. A common gesture is an upraised hand. It stands for spiritual power and helps the worshipper face evil without fear.

Use of prayer wheels is another common Buddhist ritual. They are particularly popular in Tibet. A wheel consists of a hollow metal cylinder, often decorated and mounted on a handle. Inside is a piece of paper with a mantra printed on it. Spinning the wheel is thought to be equivalent to reciting the mantra over and over aloud.

The hand gestures and prayer wheels used by millions of Buddhists have become familiar symbols of the faith. Another important symbol is the Buddha's image. It's seen in thousands of statues and paintings worldwide. The Bodhi Tree, under which the Buddha became enlightened, is another widespread symbol of the faith.

Chapter Four

SPREADING BUDDHIST IDEALS

After the Buddha's death, his followers remembered that he had urged them to take his teachings to people across India. They put all of their energies into this effort. Not long after his death, about 500 of them held a meeting. It later became known as the First Buddhist Council.

Statues of the Buddha in Bangkok, Thailand

These early Buddhist missionaries knew that they would be spreading their ideals by word of mouth. This was because none had yet been written down. So at the meeting they recited the Buddha's teachings over and over. They wanted to be sure that missionaries in various regions were all teaching the same thing.

But this unity didn't last forever. The Second Buddhist Council took place in the 300s B.C.E., about a century after the first. By that time, disagreement had set in. Traditionalists, who called themselves the Elders, had not changed their views of the Buddha's teachings. But some members of the faith had come to interpret the

Religious Tolerance

Once a merciless conqueror, King Ashoka Maurya changed his ways and embraced Buddhism. He also strongly urged religious tolerance. Such respect for people having different religious views remains a principle of Buddhism today. "It is better to honor other religions," Ashoka said. "By so doing, one's own religion benefits, and so do other religions, while doing otherwise harms one's own religion and the religions of others. ... One should listen to and respect the doctrines professed by others."

Buddha's teachings slightly differently.

This difference of opinion created a split in Buddhist ranks. The group that promoted new interpretations of Buddhist ideals later became known as Mahayana. The Elders' group later became known as Theravada. Over time, other splinter groups broke with Mahayana Buddhism and Theravada Buddhism. Eventually there were dozens of schools of Buddhist thought.

The next major event for Buddhism occurred about a century later. King Ashoka Maurya, a ruthless conqueror, invaded the Indian kingdom of Kalinga, killing at least 100,000 people.

Then, quite unexpectedly, Ashoka had a change of heart. Seeing the suffering he had caused, he was overcome with sorrow. He wanted to make amends. Hearing that Buddhism sought to eliminate suffering, he converted to the faith.

Ashoka became a major champion and promoter of Buddhism and its ideals. First he introduced the concept of dharma, meaning "moral law." He defined it as trying always to be kind, generous, and honest. At the

King Ashoka

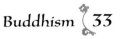

same time, he said, people should avoid cruelty, anger, jealousy, and violence. He also banned the slaughter of animals, calling it cruel.

Finally, and most significant, Ashoka sent missionaries to spread the faith far and wide. They introduced Buddhism to large parts of Southeast Asia. Over time Buddhism spread to China, Korea, Sri Lanka, Burma, and Japan. Far to the west, it even reached Iran and Afghanistan. In about 600 C.E., Buddhism arrived in Tibet, in the mountains of south-central Asia. By that time its members numbered in the tens of millions.

During the centuries in which Buddhism expanded, its ideals were finally written down. They became the faith's sacred writings. Also during this period, Buddhist monasteries, shrines, and temples were built in many lands. These became important symbols of the faith. The temples were also places for monks to conduct ceremonies and for all Buddhists to meet and pray.

Some shrines and temples have a distinctive basic form. Called a stupa, this dome-shaped structure is usually made of bricks or stone blocks. Often the bricks and stones are plastered and painted or covered in gold plates. Inside many shrines are relics, objects having special significance to the faith. Among these are bones, hairs, and other body parts thought to belong to the Buddha or his

The Great Stupa

One of the most famous and most revered Buddhist shrines is the Mahastupa. Located at Sanchi, in northern India, it rises to a height of 54 feet (16.5 meters) and is 120 feet (37 m) wide. Its central mass consists of thousands of stone blocks. Their outer surfaces are plastered and painted.

main ancient followers.

Some temples consist of a large, highly decorated stupa. The Mahastupa—Great Stupa—in north-central India is a famous example. However, in some regions Buddhists first erected a stack of tiers—levels or stories. Then they placed the rounded stupa on top. The result

The Giant Buddha statue was built into a cliff in Leshan, China.

was a tall structure usually called a pagoda.

At first none of these shrines and temples housed statues or other likenesses of the Buddha. At the time, Indian artists of all kinds didn't represent divine figures in their artworks. But during the first century C.E., this started to change. Soon statues of the Buddha appeared by the thousands across Asia. Some were huge. Biggest of all is the Leshan Giant Buddha in China. Carved from the side of a cliff in the 700s, it towers at a height of 233 feet (71 meters). In the same century, a 52-foot (16-m) bronze statue of the Buddha was erected in Japan. These great monuments remain dramatic reminders that Buddhism has a long and proud history.

Chapter Five

MEETING MODERN CHALLENGES

As it entered the 20th century and the modern world, Buddhism faced several challenges. Of the two most difficult, the first was unity. The faith had split into several groups over the centuries. Many Buddhist leaders realized that division can lead to weakness.

Women study Buddhism for several years to become nuns, just as men do to become monks.

They realized there was a clear need for these groups to reach out to one another.

A second great challenge was attacks on Buddhist leaders and the faith in general. Dictators and aggressive governments have viewed nonviolent Buddhists as easy targets for persecution. Buddhists continue to face this challenge today.

The first challenge—unity—came about partly because of the differences that had developed among Buddhists around the world. By modern times, the faith had developed three major divisions. Each had certain

A Buddhist monastery in Nepal

unique beliefs and recognized particular sacred texts.

The oldest group, Theravada Buddhism, is the most conservative. Its members view only their *Tipitaka* as sacred. They emphasize the merits of withdrawing from the world to meditate and seek enlightenment. Monks are highly respected among Theravadans. In fact monks are central to an important distinction of Theravada Buddhism. This is the idea that only devoted monks can attain nirvana.

Mahayana Buddhists are more moderate. They believe that anyone can achieve nirvana. Mahayanans don't agree on how to do this. So this branch of Buddhism is divided into several smaller sects, each emphasizing a different approach. The most prominent are Zen Buddhism, Pure Land Buddhism, and Nichiren Buddhism. However, Mahayana Buddhists have more similarities than differences. They all recognize more sacred texts than Theravadans do, including the *Mahayana Sutras.* They also have more rituals and celebrations than Theravada Buddhists do.

The third major Buddhist group is Vajrayana Buddhism, also called Tibetan Buddhism. Religious teachers known as lamas are greatly respected in this branch of Buddhism. Highest of all in rank and holiness is the Dalai Lama. Vajrayana Buddhism began as a splinter group from Mahayana Buddhism. Thus the two share many beliefs and rituals.

However, Vajrayanists have developed some unique rituals and sacred or semidivine figures. Among these figures are the Five Victorious Buddhas. According to the faithful, each possesses certain good traits that overcome a specific evil. Vajrayana Buddhism also recognizes many Wrathful Deities. Although their outward forms are hideous, they are thought to protect humans by scaring away evil spirits.

These three groups remain the largest Buddhist

Promoting Friendship Among Buddhists

An important global Buddhist organization is the World Buddhist Sangha Council. It was established in Sri Lanka in 1966. Its membership includes representatives from all three major Buddhist sects. The council's main goal remains to define and stress the beliefs that all Buddhists share. It's hoped that this will help to maintain friendly relations among the various Buddhist groups. The council also seeks to educate non-Buddhists about Buddhist beliefs and practices.

branches. Together they include about 370 million worshippers. This makes Buddhism the fourth largest religion in the world.

Although the Buddhist branches remain separate, in recent times they have tried to find common ground. A big step in that direction was the creation of the World Fellowship of Buddhists. It was established in Colombo, Sri Lanka, in 1950. Buddhists of all sects met and agreed on several shared goals. They included maintaining unity among Buddhists, treating members of all groups as brothers and sisters, and performing humanitarian acts for both Buddhists and non-Buddhists. Today the fellowship has offices in 35 countries.

Buddhists celebrate the Buddha's birthday by praying at a temple in Bangkok, Thailand.

Leaders of the WFB have often criticized attacks on Buddhists and the suppression of them. Such assaults are the second major challenge facing Buddhism today.

The Dalai Lama

The brutal crackdown on Buddhist monks in Burma in 2007 and 2008 is a well-known example. Other Buddhists have been persecuted since then.

The most famous case is that of the Dalai Lama and his followers. The current Dalai Lama was born Tenzin Gyatso in 1935. When he was a child, Tibetan monks determined that he was the reincarnation of earlier Dalai Lamas. He became the leading figure in Tibet. Because the Dalai Lama is the highest ranking Tibetan Buddhist, he is widely revered among the members of that sect. Buddhists in other sects strongly respect him, both as a leader and a human being.

Communist China seized control of Tibet in 1959. The Dalai Lama and almost 100,000 of his followers were forced to flee. They set up a government in exile in Dharamsala, India. Since then the Dalai Lama has waged a nonviolent campaign to end Chinese occupation of his country. For his heroic efforts, he received the Nobel Peace Prize in 1989.

As part of his campaign, the Dalai Lama has appeared on many TV programs in Great Britain, the

United States, and other nations. He's a pleasant person with a keen sense of humor. That has made him a sort of goodwill ambassador of his faith. Hearing him speak, many non-Buddhists have come to understand why Buddhism has attracted so many followers over the centuries.

TIMELINE

563 B.C.E.	Traditional year of the birth of Siddhartha, who become the Buddha
485 B.C.E. to 475 B.C.E	Following the Buddha's death, his leading followers hold the First Buddhist Council
380 B.C.E. to 370 B.C.E.	The Second Buddhist Council takes place
260 B.C.E.	Indian king Ashoka Maurya converts to Buddhism
200 B.C.E. to 200 C.E.	The *Tipitaka* and the *Mahayana Sutras* are completed
First Century	Buddhism arrives in China; statues of the Buddha begin to appear
Sixth Century	Buddhism reaches Japan
Eighth Century	The Leshan Giant Buddha is erected in China
1950	The World Fellowship of Buddhists forms in Sri Lanka
1959	The Dalai Lama and his followers flee after the Chinese takeover of Tibet
2007	The generals running Burma attack, arrest, and jail many Buddhist monks who had protested government abuses
2008	Buddhist monks in Vietnam raise $15.2 million to aid poor people and disaster victims

In 2008 several of the Buddhist monks arrested in the 2007 protests in Burma were tried in court. They received prison sentences of six years or more for committing so-called crimes against public order.

During the centuries in which Buddhism spread across Asia and beyond, it almost died out in India. There Hinduism remained the main religion.

The *Tipitaka* is such a large collection of writings that some modern versions have up to 50 volumes. Buddhist publishers make it available for free.

Many Buddhists recognize the five aggregates—the aspects of human appearance. They are perceptions, sensations, material makeup, consciousness, and mental conceptions.

The Bodhi Tree under which Siddhartha gained enlightenment was a species of fig tree. The tree currently standing at Bodh Gaya, the site of the Buddha's enlightenment, was probably grown from a cutting of a bodhi tree in Anuradhapura, Sri Lanka. The tree has been continuously documented for more than 2,000 years. It is said to have been planted as a cutting of the original Bodhi Tree.

The 1997 movie *Seven Years in Tibet* won a Political Film Society, USA Award for Peace. The movie, starring Brad Pitt, told the true story of Heinrich Harrer, an Austrian mountain climber who became friends with the Dalai Lama at the time of China's takeover of Tibet.

GLOSSARY

bodhisattva—someone who has become enlightened but chooses to stay in society and help those who are still suffering

compassion—feeling of sympathy for and desire to help someone who is suffering

dharma—"moral law"; striving to always be kind, generous, and honest

disciples—followers

enlightenment—achievement of great understanding and wisdom

intoxicants—substances that diminish one's physical or mental control

meditation—concentration method that empties the mind of thought

missionary—person who tries to persuade people in other countries or regions to adopt a religion

monastery—building in which devoutly religious people lead quiet, regimented lives

monk—priest or other religious person who receives religious training in a monastery and lives according to religious rules

nirvana—state of existence in which a person is freed from the cycle of life, suffering, death, and rebirth

nuns—girls or women who receive religious training in monasteries and live according to religious rules

persecuted—continually treated in a cruel and unfair way

philosophy—view of life and society

reincarnation—rebirth of a person's soul in a different body after death

relics—objects of importance or value to members of a religious group

stupa—domelike architectural form used in shrines and temples

sutra—teaching or saying of an important person

tolerance—respect and fair treatment for people having different religious views

FURTHER REFERENCE

Nonfiction

Bowker, John. *World Religions*. New York: DK Publishing, 2003.

Ganeri, Anita. *The Tipitaka and Buddhism*. North Mankato, Minn.: Smart Apple Media, 2003.

Wangu, Madhu B. *Buddhism*. New York: Chelsea House, 2009.

Wilkinson, Philip. *Buddhism*. New York: DK Publishing, 2003.

Fiction

Allende, Isabel. *Kingdom of the Golden Dragon*. New York: HarperCollins, 2004.

Coatsworth, Elizabeth. *The Cat Who Went to Heaven*. New York: Macmillan, 1958.

Koja, Kathe. *Buddha Boy*. New York: Speak, 2004.

Muth, Jon J. *Zen Shorts*. New York: Scholastic, 2005.

Internet Sites

FactHound offers a safe, fun way to find Internet sites related to this book. All of the sites on FactHound have been researched by our staff.

Here's all you do:

Visit *www.facthound.com*

FactHound will fetch the best sites for you!

INDEX

ABOUT THE AUTHOR

In addition to his acclaimed volumes on ancient civilizations, historian Don Nardo has written about the origins, history, beliefs, and cultural impact of several major religious groups and movements. Nardo lives with his wife, Christine, in Massachusetts.